# REGALOS DE LA ISLA

## *(Gifts From The Island)*

J. R. GARRY

Copyright © 2013. Garry, J. R /Revolutionary Stew

All rights reserved. No part of this production may be reproduced or transmitted in any form without the written permission of the author.

ISBN-13:
978-0615913988

ISBN-10:
0615913989

Cover photo by J.R. Garry © 2013
Spanish Language Editing by M. Nolan

# DEDICATION

For Cuba and the many kindnesses extended to me by the
communities of Trinidad, Cienfuegos and Havana.

J. R. GARRY

Mind warm, stomach full
In the 3 star version of
My supposed home.
Here, where the streets are paved
With dust and musicians,
We sit sipping the sounds
Of humming generators
And foreign languages.
You can do this,
You have "don'ts".
The air is heavy on your forehead
Hands tied, bows tied
The conspiracy of contradictions
The changes that we desire
Sweat pours from my pen,
The Hemming-way
The milky way- moon in partial crescent
Mind fertile and absent
Ron con hielo

# Trinidad Day Trip

### 10.8.13- Trinidad de Cuba

Its art in the park,
Movimiento y cultura
This is rebirth.
The weight of the aire
Is all that was needed
To break the chains of dissatisfaction.
They call me to this particular destination
Their dark stares
Are no challenge to
My inner light.
The clock starts and
The sun shines, sonrisa,
Sonrisa.
The sun will set here
It just sets me free
This is enlightenment
A gift of destiny
We'll nurse this aging dog to health
With preparations for more secretos
Hacemos mucho contigo… invasor

# Por la Noche

### 10.8.13 - Trinidad de Cuba

La verdad es verde
Como las montañas en la isla,
Mi isla.
A solid performance of self
Salud y revolución para todos.
Warm smiles and contented bellies
Always with a day break.
Mortgage a physician
So you can keep the lights on
And the tourists sip cocktails
Under chandeliers and tobacco smoke.
Con salud y revolución
Con mucho gusto.
Si, los habitantes sonríen
The Hemming-way
Drifty and noncommittal your
Visitors stand, or sit, with straws in the air
Oh, unaffiliated and self defined
Unite in peace and confidence.
No makeup, bowtied, no bra Saturdays
With a salsa of creative energy
And a knack for honoring physical and mental health.
A way of being.
A fiesta, but not apart-
More an Herbal Tea.

## Untitled 1

### 10.8.13 - Trinidad de Cuba

This is the beginning

For all that is, was and will be

Niños y niñas

This rhythm is a

Buena vista

The future, el futuro es una

Buena vista

We'll stop, sit and listen

Hands and feet moving

Just as swiftly as need be

Para ti, para mí

# Noche y Vida

### 10.8.13 - Trinidad de Cuba

8th of octubre

Ocho de October

Guero, majo, hombre

Listo para todo y

Estos, siempre.

Están listos?

Noche y vida

Estamos Listos

# Untitled 2

10.9.13

Sí, como no,

No hay luz, pero fuerza

No hay agua corriendo, pero fuerza

Hay justicia y sonrisas y fuerza

Con gusto y orgullo

Esta fuerza

Es rural y hay fuerza

Hay idiomas e ideas más diferentes o variables

Pero fuertes

Este es un paisaje, es una cultura

Es un tipo que vive

Es Fuerte

# La Zorra y El Cuervo

10.10.13 – Havana, Cuba

With the godfathers, grandfathers
And the middle of the road I sit
Hedging and hemming my west bets
On this Caribbean nation
Full of communion and
Salud-
Spit salad of bebidas
Para las niñas, cuando
Empiezo otra vez
It is from the beginning of the end-
And my mind races along
Fogged and bemused,
I dream of Jeanie,
The same state of affairs
Without "A Current Affair"
"La Siete", mi mujer de
Intoxicación
The youth of my arid spring, summer, almost fall
Get back up, sit up straight, remember the Maine and many
Razones que yo venía
Shoulders held and breath released
All this distraction is really
My own peace or piece-
Of the one,
The morning moon and midnight sun
The crow and the fox

# This is Salud

### 10.10.13 Havana, Cuba

Spelling bees over jazz conversations

This is rum stimulation

No one asks questions when

You are being true to you and to them.

This bounce beat,

No need for reading glasses

The government needs to see this

Pleasant exchange.

The people to people,

A multi musician harmony.

You didn't split party lines to drop slavery

But when it comes to keeping us all healthy

You sit idly.

## Untitled 3

### 10.10.13 Havana, Cuba

The jazz record with my poetry

Sweet lines from sugar cane fields

And bus rides.

Is it now my island,

This place I am allowed to be free.

Bow tied and politically speaking-

Strong body and heart-mind believing.

This connection is satisfaction,

Saxophone-ation.

Salud y orgulloso.

Windowless and willing

To construct a new nation under this-

Our sun – for all,

Humankind.

Poems=food, songs=education

Same foundation and connection.

Our youth, always where we are.

Tell me about life, love and the world you know,

¿Qué piensas tú?

Sí, es una pregunta, pero muy difícil,

Think, think about it

# Al Parque (Fraternity Park)

### 10.12.13 Havana, Cuba

Revolutionary corners

With a growth in the center.

We all gave the best our own

For the betterment of all.

The wise, the ignorant,

The old and young, the living and the dead.

These spirits that wander

Our country are alive.

The family we forget we have,

The lost and found

Are treasured like the day of their first light

Hasta Siempre,

Es un mundo muy maravilloso

## Plaza Vieja

10.12.13 Havana vieja, Cuba

This place, calming my inner shake,

The shoulders back

The artist within, without limits

Broken lines on the edge of page perception

Inside and out – amazed.

Drowned in all the flowers of thanks

Onward we are blessed

Bienvenido a tu isla.

No hay conejos

Hay ron negro,

This old city with new spirit,

dulce y cubano

Heads up, nothing falling,

All is lifted by its own will-by the scruff,

No begging,

The ways of which our family has forgotten.

The children are taught to dance and work,

And in that order.

Pride pools and joy showers,

Meals of déjà vu.

## El Dia y Mi Gente - (El prado con Milton)

### 10.12.13 - Havana, Cuba (el prado)

En la camina, como "la rambla"

Este es un dia para mi gente

En el prado, como mi ciudad

Este es un dia para la corazón

    When we look back

    At what we learned

    It will be people and love

    This is a day we will remember

Cuando joven, cuando viejo

Cuando triste, cuando contento

Mis momentos muy raros

Las palabras que yo no recuerdo

Como chicos, como chicas

Que yo no recuerdo

Pero yo recuerdo el amor

Todos los dias de mi vida

    Here we sit, waiting for

    Words to manifest

    In the city, on the prado

Este día, este...para...

    Mi gente

## $16.75

### 10.12.13 Havana, Cuba (café Lite)

Its this moment with

Rum covered ice and

Less than what I imagined

But its el turismo que yo quiero

Por un momento.

I eat, I breathe,

We live, we never really die.

When you live as a target

You die as a target.

My face, buried in a page

Muy elegante, muy hermoso

The wind and the willows

Tú recuerdas, con justicia

# Café Lite!

### 10.12.13 Havana, Cuba

This will remain,
Esto se quedará.
Whilst we stand in our
Own quicksand of governing,
This wind will carry my voice.
Déjame entrar en la casa de justicia,
Me encanta mi isla.
Follow me where there is
No air, under the earth
With dust and a molten core.
To me, there, below, within
There is more.
Dancing under a star lit sky
The attention to details,
The conversations with our
Compadres del sur.
The words we speak
These years just before the revolution
Are most precious to me.
¿Quieren bailar?
This anticipation of the death
Of a sick, sad system.
Un emoción, un momento,
Under the same sun.
La misma luna,
Ahora quedamos
Con justo y amor.
Estos momentos son especiales.
Café cubano,
Hot, short, strong and amazing.
These moments, estos momentos
Cerca de mi mujer de paz,
De justicia, con anticipación y gratitud,
She deserves nothing short
Of an ovation of angels.
Like the tide change,
Sutil and fuerte.

# The One Eyed Cat

### 10.12.13 Havana Cuba (The one eyed cat)

## J. R. GARRY

I thank you, Hampton
The young eager son
I left too soon.
I remember you now
Like the Maine, like
A broken ship  destined to the sea floor.
I spent love dollars on you,
I did not love the hours with you.
Fist handled swords,
And a stiff breeze
An oncoming headache
And a beautiful woman
Forced to watch you,
Care for you when my mother died
You lovely one eyed asshole.
Unable to shit straight, sit straight or act right.
At the one eyed Saturday mistake.
Hoping for the conversation of a Cuban woman
Your uncomfortable presence,
A masterful revisitation,
And a sad recitation.
My one eyed old friend
We were not close,
And for a time you were wished
Great harm.
Gracias, for all your lessons,
I wish you well, you
Little asshole.

## ABOUT THE AUTHOR

**John R. Garry** is a brother, uncle, godfather, friend, poet and licensed psychologist living and working in California. He believes that he is the luckiest man in the world for all the great people he has come to know and love in his life. When he is not writing for Revolutionary Stew or working you can find him listening to music, dancing in his kitchen or enjoying in the ocean.

www.ingramcontent.com/pod-product-compliance
Lightning Source LLC
Chambersburg PA
CBHW070752050426
42449CB00010B/2439